Piers

- Most piers are free [...], and a few are lighted and have restrooms; piers may even sell bait and tackle. Most are bare-bones affairs, and you'll need to bring all your gear and bait with you.

- Some piers may charge a small daily fee to fish. Laws vary, but on most piers you'll need a saltwater fishing license.

- For more success, watch for when and where locals go fishing. In some seasons, night fishing might be best.

- As for gear and bait, take note of the water habitat of the pier. If it's over a rocky shore, rig your gear for fish that feed on barnacles and crabs. If it's built atop sand, use a surf rig. And don't forget to try your luck under the pier; some fish take shelter right around the pier pilings.

- When in doubt, ask around, as local knowledge can be a great help.

Surf

- Before you hit the beach, visit a bait shop for advice.

- When surf fishing, any rod will work, as long as it can handle a 2–4 oz. sinker.

- Large 10–15 foot-long rods are used when long casts are needed to reach fish, but fish often feed just at the beach line.

- Even small surf fish are strong, so anchor your rod well. (Don't try to use a cooler, or you might lose your gear.)

- Most surf fish have sharp teeth, so attach a strong leader below the weight. Use a short one when in rough surf and a long one when waves are smaller. You want enough weight in your leader so it doesn't roll down the beach, but it needs to be light enough to roll in the surf.

- An outgoing tide is commonly thought to be the best fishing, but on beaches with a deep ledge, an incoming tide is often better. Wherever you're fishing, fishing with a tidal current is better than with a slack tide.

- Bring pliers and gloves. Some fish have sharp teeth!

average catch size

Red Drum

Surf, shell bars and weedy flats

Dark spot at base of tail above lateral line; snout protrudes beyond lower lip

14–20"
3–8 lb.

SALTWATER • BRACKISH

Black Drum

Bays, estuaries and channels

4–5 wide vertical bars; horizontal mouth with many chin barbels

20–24"
15–20 lb.

SALTWATER • BRACKISH

Freshwater Drum

Lakes and slow streams

Lateral line runs from head through tail

10–12"
2–5 lb.

FRESHWATER

Gray Triggerfish

Rocks and reefs

Leathery skin; the first dorsal spine can lock into a vertical position

10–12"
1–2 lb.

SALTWATER

Hybrid Striped Bass

Saltwater, but introduced to lakes and rivers

Two tooth patches, one on back of tongue

15–20"
8–10 lb.

SALTWATER • BRACKISH • FRESHWATER

average catch size

Gulf Kingfish

Surf to deeper water

Single barbel
under chin;
upper tail
lobe short and
slightly pointed

SALTWATER

9–12"
¾–1 lb.

Spotted Sea Trout

Grass and shell flats

Dark spots over
body and
fins; inside of
mouth orange

SALTWATER

12–15"
2–3 lb.

Sand Sea Trout

*Deep bays and channels over
a sand or shell bottom*

Large eyes;
yellow-green
back; sharp
canine teeth

SALTWATER

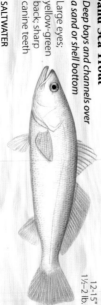

12–15"
1½–2 lb.

Gray Snapper

Mangroves and flats

Dark stripe from
snout through
eye; rounded
anal fin

SALTWATER • BRACKISH

10–12"
1–2 lb.

average catch size

Needlefish

Most shallow water areas connected to saltwater

Lower jaw longer than upper jaw

10–12"
8–16 oz.

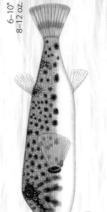

SALTWATER • BRACKISH • FRESHWATER

Puffers

Near rocks and reefs

Sloping forehead with crescent-shaped marks under eyes

6–10"
8–12 oz.

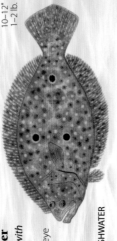

SALTWATER • BRACKISH

Gulf Flounder

Shallow water with hard bottom

The three dark eye spots on back form a triangle

10–12"
1–2 lb.

SALTWATER •
BRACKISH • FRESHWATER

Spadefish

Rocks and reefs

3–6 dark bands; rear dorsal fin matches anal fin

8–12"
1–2 lb.

SALTWATER

average catch size

Flathead Catfish

Deep lakes and rivers

Broad, flattened head with a pronounced underbite

FRESHWATER

20–28"
15–20 lb.

Bullheads

Shallow water of lakes and slow streams

Rounded tail and a pronounced overbite

FRESHWATER

9–10"
¾–1 lb.

Bowfin

Weedy lakes and streams

Continuous dorsal fin; bony plates covering head

FRESHWATER

12–14"
3–4 lb.

Alligator Gar

Slow, warm rivers

Short broad snout; two rows of teeth on each jaw

FRESHWATER • BRACKISH

4–5'
60–80 lb.

Longnose Gar

Quiet waters of larger rivers and lakes

Long, thin snout; long, narrow body

FRESHWATER • BRACKISH

18–24"
3–5 lb.

average catch size

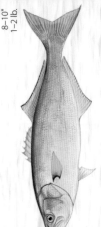

8–10"
1–2 lb.

18–24"
5–10 lb.

20–26"
4–6 lb.

10–12"
1–2 lb.

Bluefish
Surf and channels

Large mouth with sharp teeth; anal fin same shape as rear dorsal fin

SALTWATER

Great Barracuda
Shallow reefs and grass flats

Dark blotches on lower sides; large, sharp teeth

SALTWATER

Common Snook
Mangroves and grass flats

Large, flattened head; black lateral line

SALTWATER • BRACKISH

Striped Mullet
Shallow coastal waters

Large mouth with sharp teeth; anal fin same shape as rear dorsal fin

SALTWATER • BRACKISH • FRESHWATER

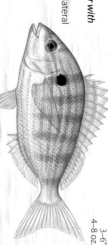

average catch size

Pinfish

Shallow water with structure

Dark spot on lateral line above pectoral fins

SALTWATER

3–6"
4–8 oz.

Pigfish

Shallow coastal waters over a mud bottom

Many bronze bars on upper body; small mouth with thin lips

SALTWATER • BRACKISH

4–8"
1–2 lb.

Black Margate

Shallow coastal waters over a rock or shell bottom

All fins black

SALTWATER • BRACKISH

12–18"
2–5 lb.

White Catfish

Shallow, still water with good cover

White chin barbels; 19–23 rays in anal fin

FRESHWATER

10–12"
1–2 lb.

Hardhead Catfish

Water with high turbidity and low salinity

Locking venomous spines in dorsal and pectoral fins

SALTWATER • BRACKISH

5–8"
6–8 oz.

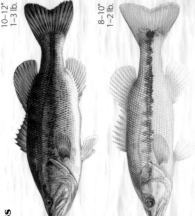

Largemouth Bass

Most lakes and rivers

Mouth extends
well beyond eye

average catch size
10–12"
1–3 lb.

FRESHWATER •
BRACKISH

Spotted Bass

*Streams and large
impoundments*

Diamond-shaped
blotches form
dark stripe on side

8–10"
1–2 lb.

FRESHWATER

White Crappie

*Deeper lakes with
open water*

Only sunfish with
six spines in the
dorsal and
anal fins

6–8"
8–12 oz.

FRESHWATER

Shellcracker

*Lakes and streams
with cover*

Dark gill spot
with a red margin

6–8"
8–16 oz.

FRESHWATER •
BRACKISH

Bluegill

*Lakes and streams
with cover*

Large dark gill
spot with a
dark margin

4–6"
5–8 oz.

FRESHWATER

Florida Pompano

Surf over sandy bottom

Deep, flat body;
blunt nose with
small mouth;
yellowish tail

SALTWATER

average catch size
10–12"
1–2 lb.

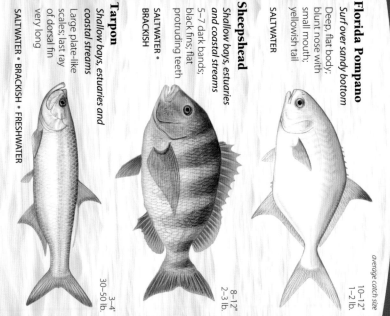

Sheepshead

*Shallow bays, estuaries
and coastal streams*

5–7 dark bands;
black fins; flat
protruding teeth

SALTWATER •
BRACKISH

8–12"
2–3 lb.

Tarpon

*Shallow bays, estuaries and
coastal streams*

Large plate-like
scales; last ray
of dorsal fin
very long

SALTWATER • BRACKISH • FRESHWATER

3–4"
30–50 lb.

Ladyfish

*Shallow coastal
waters with some
turbulence*

Very small scales;
small dorsal fin in
middle of back

SALTWATER • BRACKISH • FRESHWATER

14–15"
1–3 lb.

Lookdown

*Shallow water with
a hard bottom*

Forehead and
face are sharply
slanted

SALTWATER

6–10"
8–12 oz.

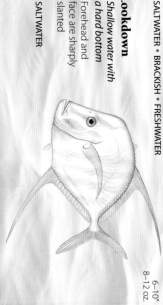

average catch size

Grunts

Shallow, rocky nearshore waters

3–5"
4–6 oz.

Small baitfish that makes a grunting sound when stressed

SALTWATER

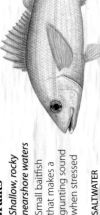

Gafftopsail Catfish

Shallow, still coastal waters

15–20"
2–3 lb.

Four mouth barbels; upper ones reach anal fins; pectoral and dorsal fin ends in a long filament

SALTWATER

Channel Catfish

Clean lakes and streams

15–20"
2–4 lb.

Anal fin is spotted and has 24–30 rays

FRESHWATER

Pickerel

Freshwater lakes and rivers

18–24"
1–3 lb.

Torpedo-shaped body; dark bar under the eye

FRESHWATER

Common Carp

Soft-bottomed lakes and streams

18–20"
2–12 lb.

Sucker mouth has two barbels

FRESHWATER

Jacks

Bays, estuaries and coastal rivers

Deep body narrows dramatically at the base of the tail

SALTWATER • BRACKISH

average catch size
16–20"
2–5 lb.

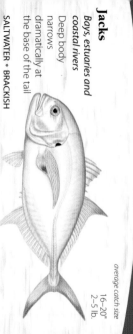

Bonnethead

Salty estuaries and bays

Spade-shaped head; tall dorsal fin

SALTWATER

24–36"
3–5 lb.

Bull Sharks

Bays, estuaries and freshwater

Stout body; rounded snout

SALTWATER •
BRACKISH • FRESHWATER

6–7'
100–150 lb.

Scalloped Hammerhead Shark

Shallows to deep water

Swept-back head with notched front margin

SALTWATER

6–7'
80–100 lb.

average catch size

Atlantic Cutlassfish
Shallow open waters

20–24"
1–3 lb.

Dorsal fin extends from the head to the tail

SALTWATER • BRACKISH

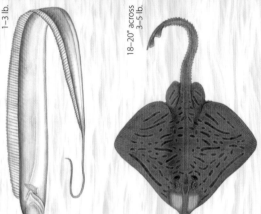

Clearnose Skate
Shallow waters with a soft bottom

18–20" across
3–5 lb.

Pointed snout with two clear spots; no stinger on tail

SALTWATER

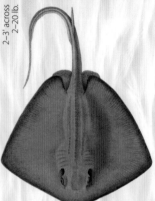

Southern Stingray
Shallow bays and estuaries

2–3' across
2–20 lb.

Midline thorns from eyes to tail; whip-like tail with a stinger

SALTWATER • BRACKISH • FRESHWATER

WHERE TO FISH: Deepwater/Offshore

Group Fishing Launches

- These boats take anywhere from a few people to as many as 50 people at one time on fishing trips; reservations are a good idea.

- Bait, tackle and fishing advice are provided, but you often have to bring your own drinks/lunch; larger vessels offer concessions. Most launches offer bathrooms, although they can be very small.

- If you're worried about getting seasick, keep in mind that the large vessels are more stable than smaller ones. If concerned, consider taking a seasickness-prevention pill an hour before you leave, and one as you get on board.

- When selecting a launch boat, ask about the ride to the fishing grounds. In some areas the ride out to the reefs is a couple hours long, and this can considerably shorten your fishing day.

- If possible, stop by the landing dock a few afternoons before you go out and see what the boat is bringing in.

- You may want to get some frozen squid and blue crabs at a bait shop to augment the cut bait usually provided.

Charter Boats

- When you're new to an area, the surest way to catch fish is also the most expensive: hiring a charter boat and a guide just for your fishing party. Most marinas and bait shops along the coast can put you in contact with charter services.

- Once you're on the water, the crews are very helpful, and there is frequently a tip pail passed before you land. On smaller boats, the captain and the mate do all they can to help you catch fish; on bigger boats you are more on your own.

- Charters provide all the equipment you'll need, and sometimes lunch. In most areas you don't need a fishing license when on a charter boat.

Rent a Boat

- If you have your own fishing tackle and boating experience, rent a boat at an area marina. Sometimes you have the option of hiring a first mate to guide you to good fishing areas.

- You'll need a fishing license, and you'll need to provide your own bait, but you'll get to be on your own. Be warned that you should know the area, keep an eye on the weather, understand buoys and markers, and have very good navigation tools. Obviously, taking off on your own can be dangerous if you're unprepared.

average catch size

Tripletail
Open water near floating objects

Rear dorsal and anal fin are set far back and rounded like the tail fin

10–14"
2–3 lb.

SALTWATER

Gulf Black Sea Bass
Open water near shallow reefs

Scales have pale centers that form faint stripes

8–10"
1–2 lb.

SALTWATER

Red Snapper
Deep reefs

Deep body with red fins; pointed anal fin

10–12"
1–2 lb.

SALTWATER

Red Grouper
Shallow to deep rock walls

Scattered white spots over pale blotches; inside of mouth is red or orange

12–15"
5–10 lb.

SALTWATER

average catch size

Vermilion Snapper
Hard-bottomed shallows

Dorsal and anal
fin margins
are yellow
orange; no
canine teeth

SALTWATER

8–10"
1–2 lb.

Horse-eye Jack
*Offshore islands, reefs
and deep holes*

Yellow tail;
protruding
scale on back
half of lateral line

SALTWATER

20–28"
2–3 lb.

Hogfish
Warmwater reefs

First dorsal spines
form three long
filaments

SALTWATER

10–12"
1–2 lb.

Cobia
*Open water around platforms,
wrecks and buoys*

Flattened head with
a protruding
lower lip; dark
stripe from
eye to tail

SALTWATER

2–3'
10–20 lb.

average catch size

Spanish Mackerel

Open water of bays and estuaries

Starting at the dorsal fin, the lateral line curves evenly to tail

16–20"
1–2 lb.

SALTWATER

King Mackerel

Open water near wrecks and reefs

Front dorsal fin blue; scaled pectoral fin

3–4'
15–20 lb.

SALTWATER

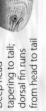

Dorado

Surface water of the open Gulf

Deep head tapering to tail; dorsal fin runs from head to tail

20–26"
5–15 lb.

SALTWATER

Bonito

Open, deep water, often close to shore

4–5 dark spots below pectoral fins; dark wavy bars above lateral line

12–14"
3–4 lb.

SALTWATER

Ballyhoo

Open water over reefs and rocks

Long lower jaw protrudes and forms a beak; large eye

10–15"
9–16 oz.

SALTWATER

average catch size

Greater Amberjack

Offshore near deep structures

Dark olive band from mouth through eye to dorsal fin

SALTWATER

3–4'
10–20 lb.

Blackfin Tuna

Open offshore water

All finlets dusky gray or black with white tips

SALTWATER

2–3'
5–15 lb.

Sailfish

Open water near reefs and breaks

Large deep dorsal fin is 150% of body depth

SALTWATER

4–7'
20–40 lb.

Blue Marlin

Open ocean

Pointed dorsal fin not as deep as body

SALTWATER

12–14'
150–450 lb.

Blacktip Shark

Open bays and offshore waters

Black tips on all fins

SALTWATER

3–5'
5–25 lb.

Fighting Ability

Some people fish to eat, whereas others enjoy the fight of reeling a fish in. This chart provides an unofficial ranking of how hard each fish species fights. Perhaps surprisingly, not all especially sought-after fish are strong fighters; popular game fish are noted here with an asterisk.

Strong

Alligator Gar	Cobia*	Pigfish
Black Margate	Dorado*	Red Drum*
Blue Marlin*	Flathead Catfish	Red Grouper
Blackfin Tuna*	Greater Amberjack*	Scalloped Hammerhead Shark
Blacktip Shark*	Great Barracuda	Spanish Mackerel*
Bluefish	Gulf Flounder*	Sailfish*
Bluegill	Hybrid Striped Bass*	Sheepshead
Bonito	Hogfish	Spadefish
Bonnethead	Jack Crevalle	Spotted Bass
Bowfin	King Mackerel*	Tarpon*
Bull Shark	Largemouth Bass*	Vermilion Snapper
Common Carp	Ladyfish	
Common Snook*	Longnose Gar	

Average

Black Drum*	Grass Pickerel	Red Snapper
Channel Catfish	Gray Snapper	Shellcracker
Clearnose Skate	Gulf Black Sea Bass	Southern Stingray
Florida Pompano	Gulf Kingfish	Tripletail
Freshwater Drum	Lookdown	White Catfish
Gafftopsail Catfish	Mullet	White Crappie

Poor

Atlantic Cutlassfish	Grunts	Pinfish
Ballyhoo	Hardhead Catfish	Sand Sea Trout*
Bullhead	Needlefish	Spotted Sea Trout*

Table Quality

If you're fishing and looking to cook your catch, the following chart outlines some of the most popular game fish for the table.

Excellent

Blackfin Tuna	Gray Snapper	Red Grouper
Blue Marlin	Gulf Black Sea Bass	Red Snapper
Channel Catfish	Gulf Flounder	Sailfish
Cobia	Hogfish	Vermilion Snapper
Common Snook	Hybrid Striped Bass	White Crappie
Dorado	Lookdown	
Florida Pompano	Red Drum	

Average

Black Drum	Largemouth Bass	Spotted Bass
Black Margate	Pigfish	Spotted Sea Trout
Bluegill	Sand Sea Trout	Striped Mullet
Flathead Catfish	Sheepshead	Tripletail
Grunts	Shellcracker	White Catfish
Gulf Kingfish	Spadefish	
King Mackerel	Spanish Mackerel	

Eaten by a Few

Blacktip Shark	Common Carp	Horse-eye Jack
Bluefish	Freshwater Drum	Jack Crevalle
Bonito	Gafftopsail Catfish	Southern Stingray
Bonnethead	Great Barracuda	
Bullhead	Greater Amberjack	

Not Often Eaten

Alligator Gar	Grass Pickerel	Scalloped
Atlantic Cutlassfish	Hardhead Catfish	Hammerhead Shark
Ballyhoo	Ladyfish	Southern Puffer
Bowfin	Longnose Gar	**(potentially toxic)**
Bull Shark	Needlefish	Tarpon
Clearnose Skate	Pinfish	

Adventure Quick Guides

Includes Saltwater and Freshwater Fish

Your guide to 67 of the most popular sport fish of the inland waters, surf and deepwater

- Includes sport fish from freshwater, brackish water and saltwater

- Organized by where you're fishing, whether inland, close to shore or deep sea fishing

- Pocket-sized format—easier than laminated foldouts

- Professional illustrations that show key markings

Improve your fish identification skills with the more comprehensive *Saltwater Sport Fish of the Gulf Field Guide*

U.S. $9.95

5 0 9 9 5

ISBN 978-1-59193-580-3

9 781591 935803

Adventure
PUBLICATIONS
an imprint of AdventureKEEN

SPORTS / FISHING / SOUTH